Copyright: John McManners
Published by Gemini Productions

ISBN 978-0-9532217-5-2

Book Design and Production: HPM Colour. 0191 300 6941

CUTHBERT and the ANIMALS

by
John McManners

illustrations by
Robert McManners

In Loving Memory of
Winifred McManners

ST. CUTHBERT AND THE ANIMALS
INTRODUCTION

St. Cuthbert is the most greatly loved of all northern saints. During his lifetime he enjoyed a remarkable relationship with the wild creatures of his native Northumbria. He also related kindly and gently to the domestic beasts that shared his daily tasks. There are many delightful tales of Cuthbert with birds and animals. He is the first English saint whose life is adorned with such charming stories. Even after his death, his cult and community continued to attract legends of the harmonious relationship between the saint and the natural world. These tales of Cuthbert and the animals reflect his spirituality and reveal his character at its most attractive.

Cuthbert was raised in Anglo-Saxon Northumbria. The prevailing culture and tradition during his childhood and early years was that of the Irish Celtic church. In 635 A.D. St. Aidan had led a mission from Iona to found the monastery of Lindisfarne and thus effect the conversion of the kingdom. This spirituality nurtured the young Cuthbert, especially after his entry into the religious life at Melrose, a daughter house of Lindisfarne.

The Celtic tradition was one of close harmony with the grain and rhythms of nature. Monks dressed simply; the habits they wore were not dyed but retained the natural colour of the wool. Bishops lived in community with other monks. The monastery was of scattered cells within a boundary wall. Communal buildings were few and of modest dimension; all were made from local materials, usually wood and reed thatch. The Irish Celtic church also had a special love for the sacred journey. This was in part because it was a missionary church, taking the Gospel to scattered communities. Celtic spirituality also sought out the wilderness for its own sake. In these lonely places the still quiet voice of God could be heard clearly and the soul could be refreshed. Such locations were sometimes known as 'thin' places, somewhere that sea and sky, heaven and earth seemed to merge amid the mists, and God himself was within touching distance.

The tales of Cuthbert's creatures are rooted in this harmonious spirit. Even in such a sympathetic context the stories stand out. The saint invariably offers a consideration and graciousness to his brothers and sisters in the animal world that is quite remarkable. The writers of these tales clearly thought them exceptional and cherished them.

The stories are not sentimental. Fish and geese are eaten; calves provide skins for the vellum of manuscripts and wild fowl quills for scribes. There is nonetheless a mutual respect that permeates the tales. The saint and the animals help each other. They find food, guide one another and together seek protection from cold and storm. Relationships are forged, broken and reconciled. Cuthbert cares for the domestic animals with which he works and for the wild creatures he encounters. They seem to recognise this and in return care for him.

Cuthbert's biography was first written by an anonymous monk of Lindisfarne. Bede used this account as a source for his amplified 'Life', a book commissioned by Bishop Eadfrith of Lindisfarne. (Bede also wrote a 'Life' of Cuthbert in verse.) Later legends concerning the shrine and Community of Cuthbert were recorded by Simeon of Durham and by Reginald of Durham. Folk tales have also grown up around the legend of the saint. Eadfrith is widely accepted as the scribe of the Lindisfarne Gospels, a book produced in honour of St. Cuthbert. It is a masterpiece of manuscript illumination and the most celebrated artefact of the Northumbrian Golden Age. Eadfrith seems also to have been inspired by the environment and creatures of Northumbria. The exuberant zoomorphic interlace and illustrations of the Lindisfarne Gospels abound in reference to the wildlife of the region that so delighted the saint to whom the book is dedicated.

The Venerable Bede is at the heart of this preservation. He brings to the writing his meticulous discipline as a historian. He records carefully sources of additional material.

He has a clear affection for the saint and the achievement of the Irish Celtic mission at Lindisfarne. Without Bede we would know nothing of Aidan or Hilda and much else of the Celtic church. Bede is of course a representative of the Roman tradition of churchmanship that regained ascendancy in Northumbria after the deliberations of the Synod of Whitby in 664 A.D. He is nonetheless clearly a collaborator with Eadfrith in the development of the cult of Cuthbert.

Bede also offers us a biblical reflection as to why we find these tales so attractive. In chapter XXI of his 'Life' Bede suggests that we lose the harmony with creation God gave to humanity in Eden because we ourselves do not faithfully and wholeheartedly serve the Creator. When a life is so unreservedly realigned with the will of God as that of Cuthbert we glimpse the Kingdom of God and there is a resonance of paradise.

This rationale is surely the essence of the best of all the stories of Cuthbert and creatures.

The emphasis is on the relationship, not on the miraculous. The tales are not fanciful but practical, down to earth and rooted in the soils and seas of Northumbria and as such they are more in the tradition of Jesus' parables and references to sheep and shepherds, fish and fisherman, flowers of the field and birds of the air. The Cuthbert tales stand at the edge of spiritual experience for most folk, but they remain credible.

The tales also take us into the wonderful landscape and environment of historic central Northumbria. Even today these regions are spectacular. There are golden beaches, curving bays, dunes and crags, stacks and rocks.

"Cuthbert and the Animals" contains one or two other stories that describe special places, each linked with particular birds. It does not seem unduly fanciful to suppose that the saint would have taken delight in these special neighbours. These links are akin to one of Cuthbert's most famous associations, that of his celebrated love for the Eider Duck. Though these sea-going ducks do not feature in any particular tale, there is a wealth of tradition, legend and later chronicle that underpins belief in this special relationship.

The tales also give us a window into the environment at the time of the Celts and Anglo Saxons. Cuthbert relates gently not only to wildlife, but also to domestic animals, the horses, sheep and cattle which recur in these stories. It is interesting to speculate on the early breeds, developed by Anglo-Saxon husbandry, with which Cuthbert would have been familiar. And we see the landscape. It is a land sparsely populated, yet teeming with life. It is a region both familiar and strange. It is still predominantly a wild and natural landscape. There are fells and forests, marshes and meres. Only a remnant of Roman road network permits fluent inland travel. And there are dangerous beasts. This is a land of the wild ox, the wild boar and the wolf.

This is the kingdom of these tales. It is a place at once political and religious, creative and spiritual. Through the gateway of these stories we can re-enter this golden age. With a step of imagination we too can once more inhabit for a time a lost world of otter and raven, of seal and eagle, of saint and scholar and of the gentle man who loved them.

CONTENTS

THE TALE OF THE WINTER SPARROW: A PROLOGUE

Long ago in the historic Kingdom of Northumbria, King Edwin sat in his great hall in York. The year was 627 A.D. and Edwin was a new king.

Northumbria had become the mightiest of all British kingdoms. It had emerged along with other kingdoms, such as Kent and Wessex, after the withdrawal of the Romans and the decline of their empire. Edwin had defeated Aethelfrith, the first king of united Northumbria and now ruled lands from the River Humber to the Firth of Forth. Aethelfrith was from the rival dynasty of Bernicia in the North, with its capital at Bamburgh, while Edwin was from Deira with a capital in York.

Edwin's Kentish wife Ethelberga was a Christian. She had come to faith through the mission to Canterbury of St. Augustine, sent by Pope Gregory in 596 A.D. She was anxious that Edwin too should become Christian. Such a development would have a major impact upon the Anglo-Saxon peoples of Northumbria, who had their own northern gods. Anglo Saxons had infiltrated Britain after Roman withdrawal and had pushed the British church westward to areas of Celtic fringe. Edwin therefore summoned his nobles and counsellors to consider this great issue. This was why he now sat before them in council in his great hall in York.

One of the leaders spoke up. He was a nobleman of rank, known as a Thane. He described the flight of a sparrow through a banqueting hall on a winter's day. While inside the little bird enjoys a few moments of light and warmth and comfort before returning to the cold world of winter darkness. The Thane told the king and his counsellors that the flight of the sparrow is like the life of a man who appears on earth for a little while and then passes on. We know nothing of what went before we came into this world or what is to happen after we leave it. It seemed to the Thane that the new religion offered a greater understanding of these matters and he therefore recommended that the council agree to accept the new faith.

The Thane's arguments carried the day. King Edwin then decided that he and his folk would become a Christian people.

This decision had an immediate and dramatic effect. Coifi the pagan priest threw down the altars of his gods. Paulinus, a missionary that Ethelberga had brought from Kent, began his work of teaching and baptising new Christians. After baptising Edwin and his court in York, Paulinus went north. In the River Glen in Bernicia he baptised many hundreds over a period of 36 days.

The story brings us to the northern area around the River Tweed. This will be the place of birth and childhood for Cuthbert, who is to be the leading figure in the rest of our animal tales. In this first story, however, the leading role goes to the most humble of Northumbrian birds. This celebrated story is drawn from the writings of the Venerable Bede. It is typical of his wonderful eye for an illustration which immediately brings the scene to life. It also serves as a delightful introduction for us. It shows the power of a tale to move the hearts of men. The story of the 'flight of the sparrow' is very simple, but it turned the destiny of a nation.

NOTES ON THE TALE OF THE WINTER SPARROW

1. The great hall was the central gathering point of Anglo-Saxon communities. It is to the great hall that the monster Grendel comes in the ancient tale of Beowulf, to wreak destruction upon the gathered people. Bede's World have constructed a replica hall.

2. The 'sparrow' mentioned here is the symbolic small brown bird. Such birds would be commonplace in Northumbria. Though there are a number of 'small brown birds' which could candidate for this role, the likelihood is that it is the House Sparrow, as illustrated, which is most likely to be seen around the dwellings of men.

3. 'Sparrows' also occupy a symbolic place in Scripture as the archetypal humble bird. "Are not two sparrows sold for a penny? Yet not one of them will fall to the ground apart from the will of your father.... So don't be afraid; you are worth more than many sparrows". Matthew 10. 29,31. N.I.V. As the simple children's song puts it:

   "God sees the little sparrow fall
   It meets His tender view
   Because He loves the little bird
   I know He loves me too.
   He loves me too, He loves me too, I know He loves me too
   Because He loves the little bird I know He loves me too."

4. The fact that the leader upon the council was able to use this illustration so effectively underlines the closeness to nature in which life in these times was lived. The story immediately connects with the listeners.

Thirlings Hall at Bede's World in Jarrow is a recreation of a small Anglo-Saxon hall.

THE TALE OF THE SAINT, THE SOUL AND THE SHEEP

Cuthbert was born around 635 A.D. in north Northumbria.

Great things were happening in the kingdom as well. Northumbria had a new king and a new church.

King Edwin had been defeated in battle and killed by pagan forces. Paulinus and his Roman mission had fled south. On the island of Iona were the Northumbrian princes Oswald and his brother Oswy. They were of the Bernician dynasty and were the sons of Aethelfrith, the first Northumbrian king. They had fled Northumbria at the time their rival Edwin gained the throne. The princes were Christians, having been brought up in the traditions of the Irish Celtic church. Oswald was determined to gain the crown and regain the kingdom for Christ.

Oswald faced his enemies at the battle of Heavenfield, near Hexham. He fought in the lee of the Roman wall, under a cross which he had raised on the battlefield. His inferior force was victorious. Oswald sent to Iona for missionaries. St. Aidan came to found the monastery on Lindisfarne.

Meanwhile Cuthbert had been growing up in the hills of the Scottish borders. He was a lively and spirited boy and took part vigorously in all the games of childhood. Even at such an early age there were one or two glimpses of the future God had in store for him. Once a playmate, in a prophetic moment, told him off for behaving in a manner unbecoming to a future bishop!

One evening, when he was around 16 years old, Cuthbert was working as a shepherd on the hills above the River Leader, a tributary of the Tweed. While he was watching, Cuthbert also offered many heartfelt prayers to God. Cuthbert often kept such faithful vigil during the night watches with the sheep.

On this night, as he watched, he had a vision of angels. He saw heaven open and angels coming down upon earth and returning to heaven. As they returned they carried with them what seemed to be a globe of fire. Cuthbert realised that this glow came from the soul of a great saint. He had been given a special vision of the death of a saint. He was watching the carrying of his soul to God by the angels of heaven. Cuthbert roused his sleeping companions and told them of this vision. The shepherds were moved to worship and to praise God when they heard the news. Cuthbert was strongly confirmed in his desire to seek the spiritual life.

A few days afterwards the shepherds learned from the nearby monastery of Melrose that holy Bishop Aidan himself had died at Bamburgh. He had died on the very night and at the very hour that Cuthbert had seen the vision of angels.

Cuthbert returned the sheep to their owners. He had decided to seek a monastery and enter the religious life.

Robert McManners 2008

NOTES ON THE SAINT, THE SOUL AND THE SHEEP

The story appears in both Bede's "Life of Cuthbert" and that of the anonymous monk.

There are differences:-

(i)   Only the anonymous monk gives us the location by the river Leader

(ii)   Bede amplifies the account of Cuthbert's nighttime devotions

(iii)   Only the monk describes the soul of the saint as being like 'a globe of fire!'

(iv)   Only Bede has the awakened shepherds being moved to worship.

(v)   Only Bede describes the impact of the vision on Cuthbert's desire for the religious life.

(vi)   Only Bede tells us that the sheep are delivered to the owners.

(vii)   Bede tells us that the shepherds learn 'in the morning' of the death of Aidan. The monk says this information came some days later.

Given that news would have travelled from Bamburgh and Lindisfarne, probably via the nearby monastery of Melrose, the earlier account of 'days' seems more likely.

Sheep were domesticated in Anglo-Saxon times and from much earlier. Some breeds preserved on Scottish islands (eg. Hebridean and Ronalsay breeds) will resemble those known to Cuthbert. (At Bede's World the recreated Anglo-Saxon farm exhibits some of these old breeds).

Predators abounded in Cuthbert's day, not least the wolf. Hence the need for watching shepherds at night.

There are a number of clear biblical resonances.

(i)   The watching shepherds visited by Angels recalls the visitation of the Angels in Luke 2 with their announcement of the birth of the Christ child.

(ii)   The theme of shepherds has deep biblical roots. It recalls David the shepherd boy who became Israel's greatest king. Jesus uses the image of shepherds in many of his parables and instances of the nature of God.

(iii)   The anonymous monk makes reference to the vision of a ladder to heaven with angels that was given to Jacob.

(iv)   There is also a resemblance to the story of Elisha and Elijah. Elijah the prophet is taken up to heaven in a fiery chariot. (Swing low sweet chariot). His mantle rests upon the shoulders of his pupil Elisha who goes on to minister and prophesy in the spirit and power of Elijah. In some similar sense we are seeing a moment of succession when the young Cuthbert is called and inspired by God to walk in the footsteps of the great saint Aidan.

The waters of the River Leader as they flow from the Lammermuir Hills into the River Tweed.

THE TALE OF THE HORSE AND THE BREAD

Cuthbert was still a youth but now his heart was set upon the religious life. He was rapidly growing into a strong young man. Before entering the monastery he travelled through Northumbria on horseback. One day upon his journey he was to receive further encouragement for his calling through a gift from God.

Cuthbert was travelling alone. He was returning home from the south of the kingdom and it was the beginning of winter. He chanced upon a village. He asked a good woman of the village for food for his horse. She offered Cuthbert food for himself also. Cuthbert was unable to accept as it was Friday and he was fasting till the evening. The good woman urged him to accept, warning him that he was about to enter a desolate area where he would be without food or shelter. Cuthbert was determined to maintain his fast. He thanked the woman kindly; then he and his horse rode on.

Cuthbert set out upon the rest of his long journey. He passed through an empty region where no-one lived. He realised that he would not complete his journey in one day. He began to look for a place where he and his horse could stay and pass the cold winter night.

Rain and storm set in. The travelling companions were hungry and weary from the journey.

After crossing the River Wear, near Chester-le-Street, Cuthbert found some rough shepherd's huts. These were deserted as they had been built for summer use only. He and his horse entered one to shelter there together. The saint tethered the horse to the wall. He gathered some loose straw which had been blown from the roof and gave it to the horse to eat. Cuthbert then began to pray and sing psalms.

The horse began to nose among the thatch of the roof. As some straw fell from the roof, there came down with it a folded linen cloth. When he had completed his prayers Cuthbert felt this cloth bundle. It was warm. Within the cloth was wrapped half a loaf of bread, still warm from the oven, and some meat. Cuthbert halved the bread and shared it with his faithful horse. They ate together and were satisfied.

So God honoured Cuthbert's faithfulness. Both the young man and his steed were miraculously provided with food for their journey while sheltering in a deserted place.

NOTES ON THE TALE OF THE HORSE AND THE BREAD

The story is written both by Bede and the anonymous monk. Bede's story is much longer and considerably amplified from the monk's sparse account. In particular the whole of the early part of the story about Cuthbert's encounter with the 'religious housewife' and his determination to sustain his fast are unique to Bede. Bede mentions an additional source at the end of his narrative. The elderley priest Ingwald, who now resides in Bede's monastery of Wearmouth, has told Bede that he got the story directly from Cuthbert himself.

There are other differences.

(i) Again the anonymous monk provides geography. It is he who tells us of the crossing of the Wear and the arrival at Chester-le-Street.

(ii) It is Bede alone who tells us that Cuthbert had already provided a bundle of straw to feed the horse. It is also Bede alone who tells us that Cuthbert shared his new found loaf with the horse.

(iii) The anonymous monk provides the straw, Bede the timescale, informing us that Cuthbert could not complete his journey that day.

The geographical references remind us that the central part of Northumbria, broadly County Durham, was pretty bleak and deserted in Cuthbert's day. Northumbria was a union between two earlier kingdoms, Bernicia to the north (roughly Northumberland and the Scottish Borders) centred in Bamburgh, Lindisfarne and Yeavering Bell, and Deira to the south (roughly Yorkshire). The land between the Tees and the Tyne was something of a no-man's land.

The 'miracle' could of course have a perfectly rational explanation. One of the 'summer' shepherds could have revisited the area, left his lunch for later and returned to be disappointed. Bede and Cuthbert both believed the provision to be miraculous. It affirmed the young man's vocation and his zeal for fasting.

The horse was widely used in the Anglo-Saxon world as a beast of burden, to pull carts and to ride. The breeds of horse would be smaller and stockier than the hunter, thoroughbreds and draught horses of today. They would be much more akin to the hardy fell ponies of which a number of ancient breeds still persist. These animals are remarkably durable and can survive harsh winters in the open as long as they can find enough fodder.

Cuthbert differs from Aidan and the earlier generation of Irish Celtic monks who walked everywhere and refused horses. Cuthbert is cleary accustomed to horseback riding from his youth and pre-monastic days (as this story indicates). He later persists in the practice probably because his great energies and zeal for the Gospel take him on long journeys to remote places.

Aidan is once given a fine horse by King Oswine (Sub King of Deira). He gives it to the first beggar he meets. Oswine is furious. If he had known Aidan would give it away he would not have given such a fine horse. Aidan gently rebukes the king. "Is not this son of Adam worth more than many horses?" he asks. The king is overwhelmed with remorse and begs forgiveness of the saint.

Illustration of Cuthbert's horse drawing down straw and revealing the wrapped loaf. Bede's 'Prose Life of Cuthbert'. British Library: Yates Thompson MS 26 *with permission*.

RED KITES AT MELROSE

Cuthbert had now firmly determined to enter the religious life and become a monk. He decided to offer himself to the monastery at Melrose. Melrose was a daughter house of Lindisfarne. Cuthbert may well have chosen to go to Melrose simply because it was near his home and it was a place with which he was familiar. There may have been another factor. At Melrose there was a fine teacher and a very holy and learned man called Boisil, who was prior to the monastery. Cuthbert had learned of him and may have wished to benefit from his teaching.

The ancient Celtic monastery of Melrose sits on the central lowland of a great loop in the River Tweed. It is a beautiful place overlooked by the distant outline of the Eildon Hills. The outer curve of the loop formed by the river is guarded by tall steep cliffs which are clothed in woodland. These cliffs seem to enfold and protect the monastery.

Cuthbert rode to the monastery gates. He gave his horse and spear to a servant and made ready to enter the church and pray. Boisil was standing at the gates of the monastery. "Behold the servant of the Lord," he cried upon seeing Cuthbert. Boisil had received a prophetic insight. He realised that Cuthbert was to be a great man of God. Cuthbert told Boisil that he wished to enter the monastery at Melrose. Boisil was delighted. When the Abbot Eata returned Boisil informed him of these events. Abbot Eata was well pleased and permitted Cuthbert to receive the 'tonsure'. The tonsure was a special way in which monks cut their hair to show that they had given their lives to God.

So Cuthbert became a monk at Melrose. Boisil was his teacher and Cuthbert a wonderful pupil. He drank no strong drink, obeyed the rules of the monastery and gave himself to reading and working, watching and prayer.

The great curve of high cliffs forms a natural amphitheatre around the monastery. This theatre is not without its players. Winds hitting the base of the cliffs are diverted rapidly upward forming powerful rising currents in which birds of prey can soar and circle.

The most celebrated of these noble birds was for many years the Red Kite. For centuries these birds looked down from the skies above the monastery. They will have seen the arrival of the young man pursuing a sacred destiny. He, in turn, may from time to time have looked up from his tasks. He would have noticed the marvellous flight and distinctive forked tail of the kite. In the joy of his early monastic life he cannot fail to have been moved by the beauty of the birds and felt his spirit soar with the lift of their glorious wings.

NOTES ON RED KITES AT MELROSE

1. This story is told both by the anonymous monk and by Bede.

2. The story is much amplified in Bede. He names as his additional source Sigfith who was an eyewitness of the first encounter between Cuthbert and Boisil. Sigfrith is at the time of Bede's narrative a monk at Jarrow, though now very frail. Eata was also well known to Bede.

3. It is Bede who gives us the location of Melrose. He also adds a reflection on why Cuthbert chose Melrose rather than Lindisfarne. He was much influenced by the reputation of Boisil as a teacher. Bede also gives us details of the exchanges between Boisil and Cuthbert and Boisil and Eata.

4. The Irish-Celtic monastery at Melrose is not the same site as the medieval monastic ruin preserved within this town on the Scots Borders. The Irish Celtic site is outside the town on private land. The site can be surveyed from a public viewing point on the semi circular cliffs which surround it.

5. The Red Kites are not mentioned by Bede or the monk and do require an imaginative leap. The site was a haunt of these beautiful birds for centuries. It would not be possible to live at Old Melrose and not to be aware of these most striking birds with their distinctive forked tails.

6. Red Kites eventually became extinct throughout Northumberland and England. They survive in their last stronghold Snowdonia. In the latter part of the 20th century the Red Kite was re-introduced with great success in selected locations. There is now for example a thriving colony in the Derwent Valley in North Durham.

Ruins of the medieval monastery at Melrose

THE TALE OF THE SAINT AND THE OTTERS

As Cuthbert progressed in the religious life as a monk at Melrose his reputation grew.

He was asked to join Abbot Eata in founding a monastery at Ripon. Here Cuthbert, despite his relative youth, was invited to become guestmaster to the monastery. This ministry of hospitality was blessed by a visitation of angels, in the guise of travellers, whom Cuthbert welcomed. Leadership of the religious community in Ripon became confused by the appointment of Wilfrid, a forceful advocate of the Roman tradition. Eata and his monks returned to their Irish Celtic house back home in Melrose. Here Cuthbert found that his beloved teacher Boisil was dying. Together they shared Boisil's last days with a study of St. John's Gospel.

After the death of Boisil, Cuthbert was invited to take his place and become prior of the monastery. He filled this role with distinction. He was tireless in his mission to even the remotest places. His holiness and wisdom were also becoming well known. He was sometimes asked to help other monasteries.

One such request came from Aebbe, who was abbess of Coldingham. This monastery was located high on rocky east coast cliffs and was home to both monks and nuns. Cuthbert was invited to visit and to encourage the community. Cuthbert travelled to Coldingham and stayed for many days.

At night he used to walk down onto the beach near the monastery to pray. One evening one of the other monks decided to follow Cuthbert and to watch him. He watched, amazed from his hiding place, as the saint strode boldly into the sea. Here amid the waters he sang and praised God throughout the night. When dawn was near Cuthbert came up out of the water. He knelt on the sand to pray.

The watching monk could not believe what happened next. Two young otters ran from out of the sea and up to the saint. They licked Cuthbert's feet. They then warmed his feet with their breath and tried to dry them with their fur. The saint patiently received this ministry. He then blessed the young animals and they went tumbling back into the sea.

The watching monk, hiding behind the rocks, trembled with fear and sorrow. He had intruded upon a sacred moment between the saint and the wild creatures.

Later that day, deeply sorry, he told Cuthbert what he had done. Cuthbert forgave him, and asked the monk to tell no-one what had happened. The monk was relieved to be forgiven and remained silent about it for the rest of Cuthbert's life. After Cuthbert's death he was no longer bound by the promise and he told the story to many people.

Robert M. Marzocca 2007

NOTES ON THE TALE OF THE SAINT AND THE OTTERS

1. Both Bede and the anonymous monk tell this story. It is probably the most famous of all the tales about Cuthbert and animals.

2. There are differences.

    (i) it is the monk (unusually) who names one of his sources. It is a priest called Plecgils.

    (ii) The monk describes the saint as going into the waves 'up to his loincloth', suggesting that Cuthbert has disrobed before entering the water. Bede is silent on this matter.

    (iii) The monk describes Cuthbert once soaked up to his armpits by a tumultuous and stormy sea. Bede on the other hand has the man of God going into the water until the swelling waves rose as far as his neck and arms.

    (iv) Only Bede names the creatures as being young otters.

3. Otters became almost extinct in England in the 20th century as a result of hunting and the use of pesticides which entered their food chain. They remained in Scotland. Otters began to reappear towards the end of the century and one of their first footholds was on the river Till in Northumberland.

4. We tend to think of otters as being river animals but in Scotland it is quite normal to find otters foraging on the coast line and in tidal rock pools.

5. The sea around St. Abbs Head is particularly rich in marine life. It encompasses undersea caves and is an area of European special scientific interest. It is a favourite venue for scuba divers. It would therefore, in Cuthbert's day when otters were much more plentiful, be a very likely spot in which to find the animals.

6. The Celtic Irish monastery was based on top of the big rock at St. Abbs Head which thrusts into the sea. There is a later medieval monastic ruin a short distance inland.

7. St. Abbs Head is called after the founding abbess of the monastery. St. Abb being a corruption of Aebbe.

8. Plunging into cold waters in order to sustain long prayer vigils was not unknown in Irish Celtic monastic communities. At Melrose a monk called Drycthelm was well known for standing deep in the river in order to sustain prayer. He was known to continue to do this even when he had to break the ice to get into the water. As he stood in the river surrounded by ice floes, companion monks would sometimes cry out "Is it not cold brother Drycthelm?" to which he would always reply, "I have known it colder".

One of the many small coves set into the great rock of St. Abbs head.

THE SAINT AND THE DOLPHIN MEAL

On another occasion Cuthbert was called from Melrose to ministry and mission in the land of the Picts, in the north of Scotland. Cuthbert set sail from Northumbria with two companion monks.

Their voyage was at first uneventful. Wind and waves were in their favour. The voyagers thought that they would be able to take advantage of these favourable seas. They planned to travel and return quickly and therefore did not carry many provisions. When they reached a region called the Nidauri, they put to shore. Here their problems began.

The travelling monks discovered that the section of coast on which they had landed was deserted. There was no prospect of provision or shelter and their own supplies were running low. To make matters worse a storm blew up. They were unable to put to sea to continue their journey, or to return home. Cuthbert and his two companions had to remain on the barren coast. They had arrived shortly after Christmas Day and the storm continued unabated for many days. Soon their food had run out and they were in great danger of dying from cold and hunger.

Cuthbert used the whole time to pray, both day and night. The monks remained trapped by the weather until the feast of Epiphany. Epiphany is a special festival day in the calendar of the church. It is the day on which Christians celebrate the visit of the wise men to the baby Jesus. Cuthbert encouraged his friends. He reasoned that there was no-one to help them; therefore, they must rely on God. Surely God would provide for them so that they to could take part in the feast of Epiphany? He urged them to search the shore. Cuthbert led his friends back to the place on the beach where he prayed every night. Here, laid out on the ground, they found three pieces of dolphin flesh, looking as if they had been prepared for cooking by some human hand. The monks rejoiced at this miraculous provision. Cuthbert knelt and praised God.

Cuthbert pointed out to his friends that God had not only provided food, he had told them when they were to be saved. The food was to sustain them, but it was also a prophetic message. There was food set out for three days. Therefore the storm would continue for only three more days.

The monks took and cooked the food, eating one portion each day. As surely as Cuthbert had foretold, after three days the storms died away. On the fourth day the seas were calm and the skies were clear. The three companions sailed back to Northumbria and a safe port, blown by favourable breezes.

NOTES ON THE SAINT AND THE DOLPHIN MEAL

1. 'The Land of the Picts'. North east Scotland was peopled by the race known as the Picts (or painted people). The west of Scotland had been infiltrated by the Scots from Ireland and in the regions we now know as the Scottish Borders there were various British tribal kingdoms. Northumbria itself at the height of its power extended to Edinburgh.

2. There is debate about the coming of Christianity to the Picts. Bede attributes their conversion to St. Columba. This view has been challenged. Certainly Columba was a charismatic and energetic figure who founded a number of monasteries in the west of Scotland. At Iona he founded a most important centre. There is a later involvement in Pictland with monks from Wearmouth and Jarrow, which is also felt to have been influential.

3. 'He came by boat'. The Anglo-Saxons were possessed of excellent sailing craft. The Sutton Hoo ship burial reveals in the ground the shape of a boat. This boat has been recreated in half size replica by Dr Edwin Gifford and his wife. The boat, known as Sae Wyfling has proved to be wonderfully sea worthy. Two other things were discovered. The size and strength of the stern oar housing suggests that the boat was driven by sail as well as oar. Also the boats have a very shallow draft and would therefore have been navigable well up river.

4. Several breeds of dolphin and porpoise are to be seen off the north east coast to this day. In Cuthbert's day they would have been even more commonplace.

5. For many years the harbour at Amble was home to Freddy the Dolphin who swam and gambolled among the swimmers and pleasure craft.

6. In our time there has grown resistance to the idea of eating dolphin meat. This seems to be a recognition of the dolphin's status as a mammal and our acknowledgement of the high intelligence of the creature. (See the story "Dolphin Gone" the first published piece by the playwright Tom Haddaway).

7. Cuthbert and the monks would consider the dolphin to be a fish. Dolphin flesh was regarded as fish by the church for some time. It therefore could be eaten during Lent.

Illustration of Cuthbert and his companions upon the sea. Bede's 'Prose Life of Cuthbert'. British Library: Yates Thompson MS 26 *with permission*.

THE SAINT, THE EAGLE AND THE FISH

One day Cuthbert was on one of his many missionary journeys from Melrose to remote parts of Northumbria. He was walking south through the hill country along the line of the River Teviot, a tributary of the Tweed. On the way he taught the country people he met and baptised those who came to faith. He had a boy for a travelling companion. The pair had been walking all morning. The journey had been long and hard and both were beginning to tire. It was still some way to the next village where they hoped to be refreshed.

Cuthbert sensed that the boy was becoming anxious. He also saw an opportunity to teach him more of the ways of God and the walk of faith. He asked the boy whether he had given any thought as to where they would find food for the journey. The lad's response revealed that he had indeed been thinking and worrying about it. He had calculated they had brought no provisions, that they knew no-one on the route and yet to fast for the whole day would be very difficult on such an arduous journey. Cuthbert was moved with compassion for the boy and spoke swiftly to allay his fears. He assured the boy that he who trusts in the Lord should never be downhearted. God will always provide for the person who is faithful.

At that moment a magnificent eagle appeared in the distant skies. Sensing that God wished to encourage the boy directly, Cuthbert pointed out the bird. "God is able to provide for us today, even through the ministry of that eagle", he told the boy.

They continued their journey. Suddenly they saw the eagle again. It was much closer and was settling down upon the river bank. Cuthbert told the boy to run and see what the eagle had brought for them. The boy ran to the river bank. The eagle lifted up and flew off at his approach. There, beside the river, lay a large fish that the eagle had caught. The boy took up the fish and ran back eagerly to the saint. "Why have you not given our fisherman his share?" asked Cuthbert. The boy understood. He quickly cut the fish in two and returned half to the riverbank. The eagle fisherman returned for his food.

Inspired by this provision, Cuthbert and the boy were able to continue to the next village, carrying their precious meal. In a friendly household they broiled the fish and all shared the wonderful food. So it was that God provided for Cuthbert, the boy, their new friends and for the eagle. All ate and were satisfied.

NOTES ON THE SAINT, THE EAGLE AND THE FISH

1. This story is told by both Bede and the anonymous monk. The stories are parallel and there is no significant additional material in either. There are however differences.

2. Differences: -

   i. It is the monk only who locates the river as being the Teviot. By journeying south Cuthbert and the youth are following the line of the river as an access into the Cheviot Hills. (Cuthbert was already celebrated for taking the Gospel to remote places).

   ii. The monk also gives his source as Tydi, the priest also mentioned as an authority for the tale of the dolphin flesh provision.

   iii. The saint in Bede's account says that provision from the eagle is possible. The monk has the saint revealing the eagle as having been instructed by God to provide food.

   iv. Each writer provides a different biblical reflection. The monk has Cuthbert quoting

   'Seek ye first the kingdom of God and his righteousness and all other things shall be added unto you.'

   'I have been young and now am old and I have not seen the righteous forsaken.'

   'The labourer is worthy of his hire.'

   While Bede has the saint utter a final benediction upon the episode 'blessed is the man whose hope is in the name of the Lord and who has not looked after vanity or idle folly.'

   v. Bede has Cuthbert refer to the ministering eagle as 'our handmaiden'.
   The monk has Cuthbert refer to the bird as 'our fisherman.'

3. The eagle could be a White Tailed Sea Eagle. These huge and magnificent birds are adept at catching large fish close to the water's surface. They would be common place throughout Northumbria in Cuthbert's day. They became extinct in England, hanging on for a time in Scotland before finally leaving the islands. Sea Eagles remained well established in the Norwegian fiords. In recent years these magnificent birds have been re-introduced into Scotland and have now become well established on parts of Scotland's west coast such as the Isle of Mull.

4. The fish must have been large as even half of it went on to feed Cuthbert, the boy and their hosts in the village. Such a large fish would probably be a salmon. The rivers of Northumbria teamed with salmon in the days of Northumbria's Golden Age. Only a salmon caught in a river would be so big. There is a subtext to the story, which is not explicitly stated. The eagle has landed on the riverbank because it cannot manage such a large fish. By cutting the fish in half Cuthbert's youth returns to him a manageable meal. So all are satisfied.

5. There is something very pleasing about the idea of sharing the fish in equal halves. It is what Bede also records Cuthbert as doing with the loaf discovered by his horse in the derelict shepherd's hut near to Chester-le-Street. It also carries resonance of the gracious conduct of St. Martin of Tours, who, when confronted with a shivering beggar, takes his sword and cuts his cloak in half giving half to the unfortunate man.

The River Teviot flowing from the Cheviot Hills into the River Tweed.

ST. CUTHBERT'S BEADS

After many years at Melrose, Cuthbert was sent by Abbot Eata to Lindisfarne. Eata had taken on responsibility for Lindisfarne as well as Melrose after the Synod of Whitby in 664 A.D. At this synod King Oswy, who had succeeded his brother Oswald, had finally resolved the tensions which existed between Roman and Celtic church traditions. Oswy decreed that, in Northumbria, Roman churchmanship would prevail. This ruling greatly hurt Colman, the then abbot of Lindisfarne. He and a number of his monks withdrew from Lindisfarne and returned to their mother house on Iona. Eata and Cuthbert, despite their Irish Celtic backgrounds (Eata had been a pupil of Aidan), did feel able to accept the ruling. Their task at Lindisfarne was somewhat daunting as the substantial group of monks who remained were feeling very bruised by these events.

Lindisfarne is a tidal island off the Northumbrian coast near Bamburgh. At low tide it is linked to the mainland by a series of mudflats and sandbanks. An ancient pilgrim's way, marked by tall stakes, crosses the flats. This island was now to become the centre of Cuthbert's ministry.

Cuthbert, who had been given the role of provost, now had to try and restore morale. There were also some issues of discipline to address. Cuthbert was used to very rigorous standards.

When Cuthbert tried to bring in new rules and establish new standards at Chapter meetings many monks tried to argue with him. Cuthbert would not argue. He simply got up and gently left the room. The next day he would come back and calmly talk again about the new rule. Gradually the monks were won over by Cuthbert's patience and graciousness.

Cuthbert kept his peace of mind at this time by spending many hours in prayer in solitary places. His favourite place was a little islet called Hobthrush Isle. This sits in a small sandy cove. A pathway runs down to the cove from the monastic site. Cuthbert must have walked this pathway many times. Hobthrush also is tidal. It is only a small way from the shore.

On the beach opposite the islet are to be found many strange stones. They are green discs with a hole in the middle. According to legend, Cuthbert used to thread these beads onto a string to make a rosary for use in prayer. The stones are known as St. Cuthbert's beads

The story is charming, but without any historic basis. The beads are not stones at all but fossils. They are fossilised sections of the stalk of an ancient sea creature called a Crinoid – a kind of anemone. Cuthbert's beads are still a found on Lindisfarne beaches by the diligent fingers of eager schoolchildren.

NOTES ON ST. CUTHBERT'S BEADS

1. There is no historic source for the legend. It is probably a folk tale, which has grown up to explain the strange beads found on the beach opposite Hobthrush. The sanctity of Cuthbert and the similarity to rosary beads would do the rest.

2. There are other legends attached to the beads. One is that they are the tears of a mermaid who fell in love with a monk who had a beautiful voice. She could not marry him, as she was not human. She died of a broken heart leaving her bitter tears on the shore to bear witness to her pain over the centuries.

3. Scott in his poem 'Marmion' does make specific reference to the beads and the legend.

4. Hobthrush is now more often known as St. Cuthbert's Isle in honour of the saint.

5. Although the anonymous monk records Cuthbert's transfer to Lindisfarne, it is Bede alone who records his island activity.

6. Scott in Marmion links Cuthbert's legend with St. Hilda.

   'But fain St. Hilda's nuns would learn,
   If, on a rock, by Lindisfarn
   St. Cuthbert sits, and toils to frame
   The sea-born beads that bear his name:'

7. Hilda too enjoys a legend linked with a fossil. Ammonites are found on the beaches of Whitby. Their coiled shape has given rise to the legend that they are serpents which the saint has vanquished.

St. Cuthbert's Island at high tide. *Photograph Robert Cooper*

THE LINDISFARNE GOOSE

While on Lindisfarne, Cuthbert used to pray day and night. Sometimes he prayed in solitude on Hobthrush Isle. At other times he used to work with his hands so he could stay awake to pray. He also walked all around the island to see how everything was getting on. As he walked he sang psalms. He slept little, sometimes going all day without sleep. Even when he was sleeping if he was unexpectantly awakened he was never angry. He used to say, "No one who awakens me angers me. He who wakes me up makes me happy for driving away the heaviness of sleep and making me think of something useful." When Cuthbert celebrated Mass he could not do it without shedding tears. When he sang he sang from a full heart. The music often broken by the sound of his sighs. He was upright and holy in his personal life. He reproved wrongdoing in others but was most kind and gracious with the penitent. He was even known during confession to break into tears, thus by his example prompting greater penitence and more complete forgiveness.

As time went on Cuthbert had a greater desire to be alone with God. He withdrew more and more to spend time on Hobthrush Isle. Hobthrush is just around a corner of Lindisfarne where the island coastline turns from the inner sand to the outer sea. This inner place is a large expanse of mud-flats and sandbanks which can be seen at low tide. Theses mud-flats are very important to wild fowl. In the winter these ducks and geese fly to Lindisfarne from places within the Arctic Circle. They come to escape the cold and to feed and shelter for the winter. The most famous of the Lindisfarne visitors is the Pale-bellied Brent Goose. Lindisfarne is their main winter refuge and is the most important site in the world for gatherings of these birds.

During his time on Hobthrush the saint would have had a panoramic view of the flats. The small outer cliff of the island gives a wonderful viewing point. Almost opposite the island is the long sandbank which is the main gathering point for the birds when the tide is out. Cuthbert could not fail to have seen these marvellous great gatherings. Nor could his heart fail to have been touched by the glorious natural beauty his loving Heavenly Father had set before him to inspire his praises and aid his meditations.

NOTES ON THE LINDISFARNE GOOSE

1. The mud-flats between Lindisfarne and the coast are an over wintering ground of international significance for the Pale-bellied Brent Goose.

2. These fowl sweep in huge numbers from their summer grounds in the Arctic Circle. They come from some of the northern Canadian islands and Svalbard, as well as from north-eastern Greenland.

3. The Lindisfarne flats provide not just a haven, they are attractive to the geese because the tidal balance of the flats is perfect for the growth of eel-grass. Eel-grass (Zostera) is the main winter food for the geese.

4. When the waters above the grass are shallow the geese feed by 'up-ending' in a manner more usually associated with ducks.

5. The geese also sometimes graze in flocks on nearby meadow land.

6. In flight Pale–bellied Brent Geese are spectacular. They congregate in huge flocks. These gatherings fly to a ripple–like rhythm of irregular giant skeins in shallow-arrow shaped formations following one another in sequence.

7. There is a closely related strain of Dark-bellied Brent Goose. The summer grounds of these geese are to be found in the tundra of Northern Siberia.

St. Cuthbert's Island showing nearby sand banks. *Photograph Robert Cooper*

THE TALE OF THE SAINT, THE BIRDS AND THE BARLEY

After many years on Lindisfarne, Cuthbert was allowed by Abbot Eata to seek even greater solitude. He longed to find an even more lonely place to be alone with God.

He joyfully looked forward to it. He rejoiced that he was now considered worthy to lead a life of divine contemplation. Cuthbert's chosen place of retreat was the island of Inner Farne.

Inner Farne is the largest of the group of Farne Islands, which lie off-shore between Bamburgh and Seahouses. There are seventeen islands but only three carry soil and vegetation. The side of Inner Farne that faces the mainland has high cliffs. On the other side the island slopes down to a sandy beach and sheltered cove, this is the only landing place on the island and must have been the place where the saint first landed. Nowadays this small landing beach is known as St. Cuthbert's Cove.

Cuthbert was a strong and energetic man. He built three houses. These were round in shape. Cuthbert made them by digging deep into the rock and then building up the walls from the rock he had removed. One house was for prayer, one for living in and a third large house for visitors. He prayed with the monks who first went with him to the island. God inspired them to dig deeper into the floor of his round house and here they discovered a well. The well filled with water every day and did not overflow. Without a well giving fresh water Cuthbert would have been unable to stay on the island for any length of time.

Cuthbert also needed food. He at first lived on bread provided by his guests. He preferred to grow his own food so he could live on the island without support. He first planted wheat in the spring. The wheat failed to grow. So Cuthbert acquired some barley and planted it, even though it was beyond the planting season. The barley sprang up quickly and produced a large crop. As soon as the barley began to ripen the birds came to eat it. Cuthbert approached the birds in the most friendly way. "Why are you eating crops which you did not sow?" he asked. "Perhaps you need them more than I do. If you have permission from God, do what he has allowed you to do. If you do not have permission go away and do not harm things which belong to someone else." At these words the whole flock of birds took flight. They never again attacked the crops.

In this way the saint was able to provide for himself and to sustain a harmonious presence on the island.

NOTES ON THE THE SAINT, THE BIRDS AND THE BARLEY

1. The story of the birds appears only in Bede.

2. Bede himself points out that it has resonance of a story linked with St. Antony, the desert father, where the saint rebukes wild asses which are eating his crop and the asses depart.

3. Both Bede and the monk mention that the Inner Farne was uninhabitable because of evil spirits, which lived on the island. Cuthbert duly drove the spirits away. This account contradicts Bede's account in his Ecclesiastical History in which he describes how, at an earlier period, Aidan would retire to the island.

4. Bede and the monk also recount a number of the tales of Cuthbert's early life on the island. These include the miraculous lifting of a great stone which previously the monks could not move and the provision by God of a timber beam for Cuthbert's latrine. The monks had tried to obtain the wood without success. Then God provided it as a piece of flotsam.

5. Bede does not name the birds who attack Cuthbert's barley. Strong candidates would be Greenfinches or even Goldfinches.

St. Cuthbert's Cove on Inner Farne. *Photograph Robert Cooper*

THE TALE OF THE PENITENT RAVENS

Cuthbert continued to work the land, to pray and praise God and to live according to the natural rhythms and seasons of the island. The Farne Islands are home to a profusion of wild life, especially to many thousands of sea birds. Such was the remarkable fellowship that Cuthbert was able to enjoy with God and His creation that his island retreat soon became a place of pilgrimage. Despite his longing for solitude, Cuthbert was always gracious with his visitors who stayed in the guest house he had built for them.

One day, while Cuthbert was digging on the land of the Inner Farne, he witnessed an incident which threatened this harmony. Among the bird life of the island was a pair of Ravens. As he watched, Cuthbert saw the two Ravens attack the roof of the large shelter he had built near the landing place for the use of his guests. The birds were tearing the thatch to pieces and taking the straw to build their nests.

Cuthbert made a slight movement of his hand to tell the birds to stop. They took no notice of the saint and carried on stealing straw from the roof of the guesthouse. Cuthbert became stern and told the birds in the name of Christ to leave the island. Without any delay the two birds left their nest and flew far away from the island.

After three days one of the Ravens returned. The bird sat down on the ground just above a furrow which the saint was digging. Cuthbert realised that the raven was sorry. It spread its wings, dropped its head and began to croak softly. Cuthbert recognised these humble cries by the bird as a plea to be forgiven. He forgave the birds freely and told them that they could return. Immediately the Raven flew off to return after a little while with its mate.

When they returned both birds had in their bills a piece of pig's lard which had hardened. They placed the pieces of lard at the feet of the saint as a gift. The birds were completely forgiven and fellowship was restored. The Ravens rebuilt their nest but did no more damage. They continued to live on the island with the saint for many years. Cuthbert became very friendly with the Ravens. He used to delight to point them out to visitors. He used them as an illustration of how God loves to forgive and restore those who are truly penitent of heart and who demonstrate this by their deeds.

Cuthbert placed the hardened pieces of pig's lard in the guesthouse. There they were used by the visiting monks to grease their boots and leather sandals.

NOTES ON THE TALE OF THE PENITENT RAVENS

1. Ravens were once commonplace throughout Northumbria. Now they are confined to more remote places such as the Cheviot Hills and the Lakeland Fells.

2. They are usually seen in pairs as they mate for life. So the story rings very true.

3. Ravens are to be no longer found on the Farne Islands but they would be perfectly possible inhabitants in the days of Cuthbert.

4. The story is recorded in the same way by both Bede and the anonymous monk.

5. The only difference is that the monk has both birds each bringing a piece of lard. Bede has only one piece of lard as a gift from both Ravens.

6. Some writers have suggested that the birds have been Crows or Jackdaws but most translations prefer to describe them as Ravens.

Illustration. A number of crows take straw from the roof of Cuthbert's guest house. Bede's 'Prose Life of Cuthbert'. British Library: Yates Thomson MS26 *with permission*

The Great Auk which would have visited the Farnes in St. Cuthbert's day.

The Puffin: The species dominating the centre of the Inner Farne now is the puffin. The island is a major breeding ground.

CUDDY'S DUCKS

During the time that Cuthbert spent on the Inner Farne, one creature became specially linked to his name. This was the Eider Duck. Locally they became known, and still are known today, as Cuddy's Ducks.

Cuthbert will have already become familiar with Eider Ducks from his time at Hobthrush Island. Rafts of Eiders are often seen floating in the bay of the islet. On the Inner Farne around a thousand Eider breed. When nesting the female will allow a very close approach rather than leave her eggs or chicks. This gives the appearance of being tame. It is said that in Cuthbert's time one duck would nest in his cell.

The saint seems to have been very fond of the birds. He set out rules for their protection during the nesting season and as such can lay claim to have made the first bird sanctuary in Britain.

Of all the creatures Cuthbert loved, the Eider is said to have been his favourite. There is no special tale of Cuthbert with the ducks. There is testimony to the relationship in the work of later writers. Reginald of Durham writes that "since the days of blessed Cuthbert (the Eiders) have been hand tame". He recounts how the birds will nest in houses, even under beds! A later chronicler writes that the birds derive their tameness from those "who by their residence have sanctified it."

After Cuthbert's death a succession of hermits lived on Inner Farne. Many were men of great sanctity, following in the spirit and tradition of Cuthbert. This is particularly true of the friendly relations they continued to enjoy with the Eider. One such resident was St. Bartholomew. He lived on the island in the twelfth century. He too notes the "gracious gentleness" of the birds and attributes this to the sanctity of the island and its residents over the years.

The ducklings, once hatched and reared, soon follow their mother in a close brood to the sea. On one occasion Bartholomew found himself called from his devotions by the attentions of a mother Eider. The bird pulled at the hem of his garment with its beak and would not be dissuaded. Bartholomew followed the duck to a cleft in the rock. Then he understood the reason for her persistence. Trapped further down the cleft was one of the chicks from her brood which had fallen and could not free itself. Bartholomew climbed down, rescued the chick and restored it to the mother.

The mother Eider and her brood went happily on their way. Bartholomew returned to his oratory having saved the bird and honoured the sacred link established by his holy predecessors.

NOTES ON CUDDY'S DUCKS

1. Neither Bede nor the anonymous monk make direct reference to the Eider Ducks. Yet the tradition of Cuthbert's love for and link with the birds is very strong.

2. The first hard record of this link occurs some five hundred years later in the writings of Reginald of Durham. Reginald was a chronicler of the life of the Community of Cuthbert and the Saint and Shrine in Durham. During this time some former Irish Celtic and Anglo-Saxon monasteries, such as Lindisfarne and Wearmouth/Jarrow were brought back into service as daughter houses to the Benedictine community which had been established at Durham. The Inner Farne too continued as a place of heritage for the Community. We therefore do pick up occasional pieces of news of these sights from Reginald's writings.

3. Reginald writes of the Eiders 'in the island of Farne there are certain creatures, which since the days of the blessed Cuthbert have been hand tame. These birds have been named after the blessed Cuthbert himself. They are so tame that they nest inside the dwelling house, where they came to the table, and constructed their nest under your bed, yes and even under the bed coverings'.

4. Eider Ducks are to be found in all the waters of the British coast in the summer months – but they breed only in the north. Cullernose Point, a coastal cliff some ten miles south of the Farnes, is said to be the southern most point of this breeding range.

5. In Iceland, where Eiders breed extensively, the breast down from the female, used to cover the nest for protection and insulation, used to be farmed to make fillings for eider downs.

6. The Bartholomew tale appears in 'Beasts and Saints', translated by Helen Waddell and published by Constable in 1934. The tale is entitled, 'St. Cuthbert's Birds and Bartholomew, the Hermit of Farne'. (pages 93-95). This title clearly indicates that Bartholomew is acting in the tradition and spirit of his distinguisehd predecessor.

Sandbars and pools in the flats around Lindisfarne. *Photograph Robert Cooper*

THE TALE OF THE SAINT, THE SEAL AND THE PSALTER

Cuthbert spent many happy days on his hermitage island of the Inner Farne. Here he could communicate directly with God. He prayed, sang praises and meditated upon the scriptures. He loved the solitude of the island. Though the isle, apart from occasional visitors, was free of human habitation it was a haven for wildlife. The strange thing was that, as Cuthbert grew closer to God, the closer was his harmony with the island's creatures. In time it seemed that their presence did not seem to mar in any way the solitude of the saint. There are a number of stories of the saint and his wonderful relations with the island's bird life. The islands have also one other celebrated group of wild inhabitants. This tale reveals the remarkable empathy which had developed between the saint and all the creatures of the islands

One day the saint was sitting on a rock beside the sea reading from a small psalter. The monks of Cuthbert's day knew all of the psalms by heart but reading was an aid to meditation. As he meditated upon the scriptures the book slipped from his grasp and fell into the waves. It sank rapidly out of sight. The saint was dismayed. Books were all hand-written by scribes on vellum and were infinitely precious. He offered immediate prayers to heaven for its recovery. A seal basking upon a rock nearby saw Cuthbert's distress. The animal slipped softly into the water and disappeared beneath the waves.

Within a few moments the head of the seal emerged from the water in front of the saint. In the creature's mouth was the missing psalter. The saint retrieved his precious book. He blessed the seal, which then turned and swam gently away.

Robert McManners 2008

NOTES ON THE TALE OF THE SAINT, THE SEAL AND THE PSALTER

1. This story is fragmentary. It is neither in the writings of the anonymous monk nor in those of Bede. The only source is an early Irish life of Cuthbert.

2. As such the tale is probably without historic foundation and is simply a charming legend added to glorify the saint's reputation.

3. There is evidence that Bede made a brief reference to the account in an early draft of his verse life of the saint.

4. The Farne Islands are of course a major breeding ground for the Atlantic grey seal. They mainly congregate on the outer Farne Islands around Longstone.

5. They frequent all the waters around the islands so there are plenty of 'suspects' for the leading role in the tale.

6. We do have an almost perfectly preserved copy of a small manuscript book of the period. When the body of Cuthbert was translated to a place behind the high altar of the new Norman Cathedral the coffin lid was removed revealing 'a text of the Gospels' lying on an inner lid. This was a beautiful copy of the Gospel of St. John bound in goatskin. The calligraphy is exquisite. The book is attributed to the Wearmouth/Jarrow scriptorium and is believed to have been a gift to the Community of Cuthbert, perhaps at the time of his first translation in Lindisfarne. It is the only Anglo-Saxon book of the period to carry its original binding.

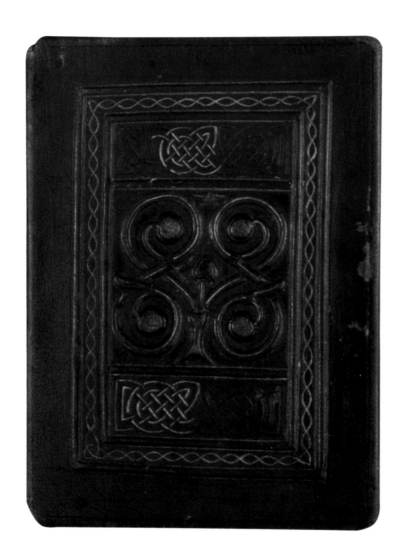

The original binding of the Cuthbert Gospel of St. John (Stonyhurst) on loan to the British Library.

ROSEATE TERNS OF COQUET ISLAND

Though now living in permanent retreat as a hermit on the Inner Farne, the demands upon Cuthbert grew along with his reputation for sanctity. He was even sometimes asked to forsake his solitude to give others the benefit of his ministry and wisdom. One such request came from the Abbess Aelfflaed of Whitby. She asked Cuthbert if he would come and meet with her to talk over matters of importance. Aelfflaed was of royal blood. She had become abbess of Whitby following the death of St. Hilda. Cuthbert had a great affection for her and for the community at Whitby.

Cuthbert and Aelfflaed agreed to meet on Coquet Island. This island lies off the Northumbrian Coast to the south of the Farne Islands. It takes its name from the River Coquet which reaches the sea at a point opposite to the island. Cuthbert came to the island by boat, sailing with some brother monks. Aelfflaed sailed up from Whitby.

She already knew of Cuthbert's goodness. At one time Aelfflaed had been very seriously ill. Even after some recovery she was unable to stand upright. She found herself thinking of Cuthbert and of his blessed quiet life. A few days later a visitor arrived bringing with him a linen girdle, a gift from the saint. Aelfflaed tied the girdle around her waist. By the next morning she could once more stand up straight. Within three days she was once more completely well.

These events confirmed Aelfflaed in her love for Cuthbert and his wisdom and holiness. At their meeting on Coquet Island she came out with the question which had been troubling her. She spoke about the life of her brother Ecgbert, King of Northumbria. She asked how long he would live and rule. Cuthbert replied sadly that the king had only one more year to live.

Aelfflaed was stricken with grief and cried many tears. Cuthbert offered words of comfort to Aelfflaed and made prophesies which foretold that Aldfrith her kinsman, then in Ireland, would be the new king. He comforted and encouraged her with many gentle words.

This important talk about the future of the kingdom was taking place in the most beautiful surroundings. Coquet Island sits like a lone jewel in the seas and is easily seen from the coast. It has low cliffs and like the Farne Islands is a haven for seabirds. The island is most famous for its nesting colony of Roseate Terns. These birds are nimble in flight and their black and white plumage is enhanced by a rosy blush on the edge of the breast.

As Cuthbert and Aelfflaed concluded their profound conversation the skies above would be adorned by an interlace of flight from these most delicate and beautiful birds.

NOTES ON ROSEATE TERNS OF COQUET ISLAND

1. The meeting on Coquet Island demonstrates the highway the North Sea represented to the coastal monasteries during the navigable seasons of the year.. Aelfflaed will have sailed from Whitby and Cuthbert from the Inner Farne. It is no accident that all the major monastic sites of the age are alongside harbours. Coldingham, Lindisfarne, Tynemouth, Jarrow, Wearmouth, Hartlepool and Whitby are all easily accessed from the sea. (Later at the time of Viking invasion this was to render these sites very vulnerable).

2. The earlier story of the gift of a girdle from the saint and the healing Aelfflaed experienced is confirmed in Bede's narrative.

3. Many of the Northumbrian monasteries had royal connections. None more so than Whitby. Hilda the founder was a daughter of King Edwin.

Coquet Island: the lighthouse incorporates medieval monastic foundations.

THE KING, THE BISHOP AND THE TERNS

Not long after the meeting between Aelfflaed and Cuthbert on Coquet Island, Archbishop Theodore called a meeting. In this meeting known, as a synod, many of the most important people in the Kingdom of Northumbria gathered. Even King Ecgfrith himself was there. The purpose of the meeting was to appoint a new Bishop of Lindisfarne. Everyone thought that the new Bishop should be Cuthbert.

Cuthbert was very reluctant to leave his solitary life on the Inner Farne. He loved the island and he loved being able to talk to God quietly, without distraction. He ignored the many messengers and letters sent to him. Eventually King Ecgfrith himself, accompanied by Bishop Trumwine and many other senior figures in the church and state arrived on the island.

They landed on the sheltered beach on the east of the island now known as St. Cuthbert's cove. In the sand and the grasses at the edge of the beach are the main nesting places for the many terns which nest on the Farne Islands. These beautiful swallow-like birds rise in a cloud if they are disturbed by visitors. If the nest sites are approached during the breeding season the birds will attack.

The saint came down the sloping grassy path from his cell to greet the landing party. The visitors knelt and with many tears implored the saint to meet with the synod. Unable to resist longer Cuthbert agreed to go with them. When he met with the synod he learned how everyone agreed that he should be Bishop of Lindisfarne. He realised that this must be God's will for his life and he accepted the post.

This famous scene on the edge of St. Cuthbert's cove is the subject of a fine painting by William Bell Scott. William Bell Scott was a well-known Newcastle artist and he painted a series of big pictures or murals for the central courtyard at Wallington Hall. In his picture of this event Bell Scott shows the skies punctuated with the hovering flight of the terns that have risen from their nests. They have been roused by their distinguished visitors and now look down upon this historic moment.

Visitors to the Inner Farne today can see the various breeds of tern in all their beauty around the margins of the beach and hovering in the skies. These are merely representatives of the many types of seabird which flock to the island. They were greatly loved by the saint. On the historic day in 685 A.D. when their companion was called away from his beloved island sanctuary it was right that, along with the kings and prelates, they too should be present.

Robert McInnersMazzers 2008

NOTES ON THE KING, THE BISHOP AND THE TERNS

1. William Bell Scott was a celebrated Pre-Raphaelite Artist. He was also, like many of the leading figures in the movement, multi-talented being also a poet of some merit. His painting is generally not regarded as being in the first rank of Pre-Raphaelite work. The remarkable series of murals which he painted for the Trevelyan family at Wallington Hall is probably his finest achievement. Bell Scott's greatest significance is his work as a teacher and advocate of Pre-Raphaelite principles in the north. He acted as a catalyst for the movement in the region. He not only influenced many young artists but he also played a major part in raising awareness of the movement among the leading industrialists and innovators. Many works by the finest of Pre-Raphaelite artists were commissioned by patrons in the north whose enthusiasm had been fired by Bell Scott's advocacy.

2. The Pre-Raphaelite Brotherhood (PRB) was founded by a group of seven radical young artists who were reacting against the artistic orthodoxy of the day. They had a particular aversion to the prevailing artistic establishment personified by the influence of the Royal Academy under the presidency of Sir Joshua Reynolds. The leading figures of the movement were William Holman Hunt, John Everett Millais and Dante Gabriel Rossetti. The society was so named because its members aspired to return to the perceived purity of art prior to the influence of the Renaissance. (Raphael of course was one of the leading artists of the Renaissance). The Pre-Raphaelites developed a style of bright colours, meticulous detail and loose perspective. Their work was initially sensational and controversial, but they gained a great champion in the critic and philosopher John Ruskin. A later Pre-Raphaelite group centred on Rossetti with William Morris and Edward Coley Burne Jones. It was from this later group that the movement in decorative arts known as The Arts and Crafts Movement was to spring.

3. Like many of the Pre-Raphaelites William Bell Scott had a turbulent personal life. He was greatly loved by Rossetti's sister Christina (painter and author of 'In the Bleak Midwinter').

The Wallington Hall Mural by William Bell Scott. *Image from the National Trust with permission.*

THE MONKS AND THE GOOSE

Cuthbert did not become Bishop straight away. He stayed on the Farne Islands for the winter. In the spring he returned to Lindisfarne and was installed as Bishop amid great rejoicing. During his time as Bishop King Ecgfrith had been killed in a battle against the Picts in northern Scotland. Cuthbert had foreseen this danger but the king did not listen to his warnings.

For two years Cuthbert served the community of Lindisfarne as Bishop. He once more travelled widely teaching people the truth of God's love for them. He performed many miracles of healing and spoke many words of prophesy.

After this time Cuthbert returned to his solitary life on the Island of Inner Farne. Cuthbert was very well known by now and he had many visitors. These visitors included monks from Lindisfarne.

One day Cuthbert came out of his cell to speak with a group who were staying in the nearby guest house. As he bade them farewell Cuthbert told the monks to eat the goose which was hanging on the wall. This goose was to provide food for visitors. Cuthbert wanted his guests to be well fed before they sailed back to Lindisfarne. The monks did have a meal before they left. They had however brought food of their own. They ate this food, leaving the goose untouched.

As they boarded their boat a fierce storm arose. This stopped them from sailing. The monks returned to the island. They remained shut up in the guest house for seven days. Outside the storm raged fiercely. They visited Cuthbert in his cell and complained of the weather. He kindly urged them to be patient. On the seventh day Cuthbert came down from his cell to visit his guests. He wanted to comfort and encourage them. When Cuthbert entered the guest house he saw the goose still hanging on the wall. Cuthbert was not at all angry. He realised at once that the storm had arisen because the monks had not obeyed him. God was teaching the monks to do what their leader told them. 'Why are you surprised that the seas will not let you leave when the goose I told you to cook remains uneaten?' asked the saint. Quickly the monks did as Cuthbert told them. They cooked and ate the goose. As the water in the cooking pot began to boil so the waves outside began to subside.

By the time the meal was finished the sea was calm. They were able to board their ship and helpful winds took them back home. They realised that God had used the saint to teach them how important it is to obey even in small things. The miracle of the storm had corrected their mistake. They had learned that God can speak to us through the words of others.

Once more visitors to the island hermitage went home having learned more of the truth of God from the ministry of the saint, the wind, the weather and the wildlife.

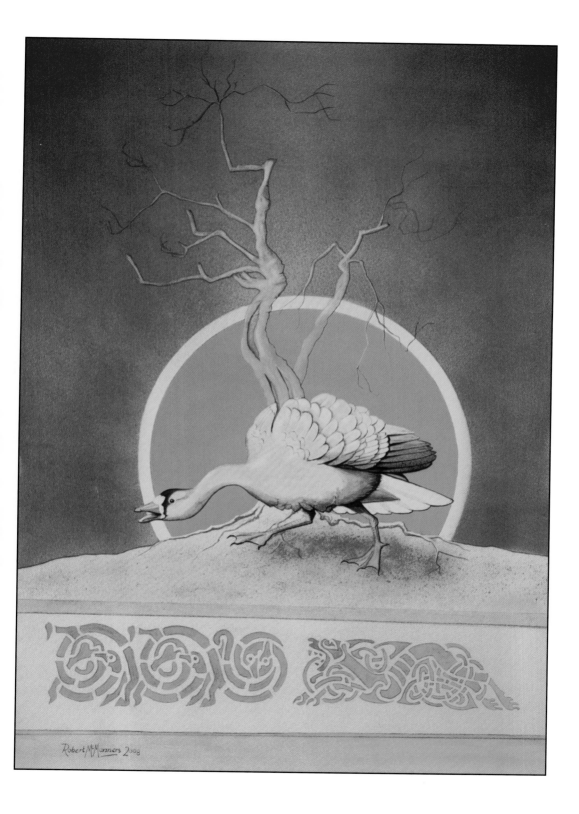

NOTES ON THE MONKS AND THE GOOSE

1. There are many types of goose which winter on the flats of Lindisfarne and nearby Budle Bay. The goose illustrated is a White-fronted Goose.

2. The story is unsentimental. The goose is to be eaten and that's that. The humble bird does play a pivotal part in the story. The food it provides is to be respected and consumed and it is not to be ignored or taken for granted.

3. The geese of Lindisfarne would provide for many of the monastery's needs not least quill feathers for the scriptorium scribes.

4. Bede gives a source for the story as Cynimund a monk and priest of Lindisfarne who is still serving in that capacity at the time Bede hears the tale from him. The anonymous monk does not carry the story.

5. The story is also interesting in that it recounts the relationship between the saint's cell and the guest house even in this latter period of Cuthbert's final island solitude.

6. The story also highlights the difficulties of sailing the short but dangerous waters between Lindisfarne and the Farne Islands. St. Cuthbert's cove, opening into a passage between Inner Farne and the Wideopens, gives a sheltered embarkation. Once out into the seas to the north, the winds, currents, waves and hidden rocks give a treacherous passage. These waters are littered with shipwrecks. The most famous was the loss of the Forfarshire in September 1838, which was the occasion of the dramatic rescue of nine survivors by Grace Darling and her father William. They rowed an open boat from Longstone lighthouse to Great Harcar rock to save the survivors.

Rock stack and cliffs of Inner Farne. *Photograph Robert Cooper*

THE EAGLE OF ST. JOHN

Cuthbert died alone upon the island of Inner Farne which he loved so much. The monks who found him lit a beacon fire to tell their brothers on Lindisfarne of his death. They then returned with his body. Cuthbert was buried on Lindisfarne. This, however, was not the end of the story of Cuthbert. Nor, even more remarkably, was it to be the end of links between the saint and the animal kingdom.

All the monks believed Cuthbert to be a saint. They decided to honour him by placing his body beside the high altar of their church. When they came to move Cuthbert they found that his body had not decayed, but was as whole and complete as the day he had died.

This was something quite remarkable. News spread rapidly and soon Cuthbert was the most famous saint in the country. Many special things were done to honour him. Bishop Eadfrith asked Bede to write Cuthbert's life story. Eadfrith himself began to write a beautiful copy of the four Gospels. This book was to become known throughout the world as the Lindisfarne Gospels.

The Lindisfarne Gospels are a quite exceptional artefact in the history of English art and culture. They are an artistic and spiritual masterpiece. They are a work of genius. The heart of the inspiration for the book is the Life of Cuthbert. The book reflects many aspects of this inspirational character. It is argued that it also resonates with the saint's love of the wild creatures of Northumbria.

In writing the Gospels Eadfrith used many different styles of decoration. These included Celtic, Anglo-Saxon and Mediterranean motif. These elements have been blended with an exquisite eye for balance and proportion.

In front of each Gospel is a portrait of each of the Gospel writers - Mathew, Mark, Luke and John. These portraits are painted in a very natural style. In this the Book of Lindisfarne is quite unlike other insular Gospel books. Portraits in other books are stylised and iconic. The portraits of the four evangelists are very lifelike. This is also true of the symbols of the evangelists which appear with them in their portraits.

In his portrait of the Gospel writer St. John, Eadfrith also gives us John's symbol, the eagle. There is no stylisation. This is surely a bird painted from life. As such this is the very first historic depiction of any Northumbrian bird. It is very appropriate that this should be the magnificent golden eagle. It is extremely lifelike and shows the feathers in exact detail. Janet Backhouse, in her essay "Birds, Beasts and Initials in the Lindisfarne Gospels", draws on the testimony of ornithologist B. Yapp to assert that "the plumage is so accurately rendered that it can hardly have been achieved save through direct observation". Yapp details the extremely accurate way in which the different types of feathers are rendered and the correct positioning of the beak.

Such a life-like painting must have been inspired by the many wonderful golden eagles Eadfrith will have seen soaring in the Northumbrian skies. In this inspiration he is at one with the spirit of the saint to whom the book is dedicated.

NOTES ON THE EAGLE OF ST. JOHN

1. In her book , "The Lindisfarne Gospels, Society, Spirituality and the Scribe", Professor Michelle P. Brown writes, "The naturalistic depiction of the evangelists contrasts with the stylised rendition in other Anglo-Saxon and Celtic manuscripts (for example the Book of Kells). There are however strong parallels with the Ezra miniature, an illustration to be found in the Codex Amiatinus, a book produced at Wearmouth/Jarrow and in the Italianate style adopted by the scriptorium of that monastery".

2. The representation of the Golden Eagle has been widely acknowledged as the first depiction of a Northumbrian bird.

3. The accuracy of the observation employed in painting the eagle has been attested to by Yapp, a leading ornithologist, who writes:

   "The distinction between breast feathers, underwing coverts and primaries is correct, and the line dividing the small feathers of the neck, which are not individually shown, from the breast is nearly in the right place. The detail of the feathers, each with a rachis and two rows of barbs (especially good in the coverts) could hardly have been invented....This eagle is in contrast to most Johnian eagles, which are merely conventional birds with hooked beaks." B.Yapp, "Birds in Medieval Manuscripts (London 1981), p.84. quoted in footnote in "Birds, Beasts and Initials in Lindisfarne's Gospel Books" by Janet Backhouse, p.168 in "St. Cuthbert, His Cult and his Community A.D.1200", ed. Bonner, Stancliffe, Rollason, *Boydel 1969.*

4. The Golden Eagle would have been commonplace in the skies of Cuthbert's Northumbria. It later became extinct in England apart from a toe-hold in the Lake District. It continues to flourish in the Scottish Highlands and Islands.

A study of a detail of the Portrait of St. John the Evangelist in the Lindisfarne Gospels showing symbolic eagle. *Study by Susan Moor*

THE CORMORANT INTERLACE

The Lindisfarne Gospels are a masterpiece of creative art. Professor Michelle P. Brown describes them as "one of the great landmarks of human cultural achievement". In seeking to analyse reasons as to why this is so, Professor Brown, as well as the sustained commitment to a high ideal, cites 'passion' and 'energy'.

These qualities are nowhere better seen than in the exuberant and endlessly inventive zoomorphic interlace which drives much of the decorative scheme. This interacts with and counterpoints the wonderful illuminated initials, which are one of the glories of the book. And there are whole pages simply of abstract decoration. These are known as carpet pages. They seem to almost come alive as the rhythms of the patterns intertwine.

Many other pages are filled with lively and brightly coloured designs which spring from the vellum to delight the reader. In these decorative panels are found a tumult of images of animals and birds. The animal shapes intertwine in marvellous ways. The shapes of the animal bodies have been stretched and changed. One shape which recurs more than most seems to be based upon the Cormorant.

The Cormorant is a most beautiful bird. It is to be seen regularly upon the rocks surrounding Lindisfarne, upon the Farne Islands and in the intervening waters. It swims with most of its body submerged and only its long and sinuous neck and head above the waves. Underwater it swims quite magically, twisting and turning in pursuit of fish. Another characteristic pose is when the bird stands on top of a rock with its wings extended to each side, hung out to dry.

The interlace ornament in the Lindisfarne Gospels seems not only to capture the image of the Cormorant but also the sinuous grace of its movement.

The Lindisfarne Gospels are the first Gospel book to make large scale use of this image. Some think that Eadfrith may have copied the idea from earlier Gospel books from Italy, rather than being inspired by the wildlife surrounding him. The Lindisfarne Gospels are however the first Gospel book to make large scale use of this image. Also the details of the Cormorant interlace show carefully noted characteristics of the bird. Cormorants have wing feathers grouped in such a way as to give an overlapping 'tiled' effect. Eadfrith paints the wings of his interlace birds with such 'scales' of feather groups in varying colours. Backhouse highlights this detail and makes a strong case for its being the product of detailed and meticulous observation. Of course these decorative motifs do not purport to be portraits. There is stylisation. Yet the similarities are such that it does seem highly likely that Eadfrith was influenced by the marvellous birds he constantly saw around his island scriptorium. Inspired by these creatures he infused some of their spirit into his decoration.

A decorated book, dedicated to the memory of Cuthbert would surely be incomplete without reference to the seabirds of his beloved islands.

NOTES ON THE CORMORANT INTERLACE

1. The Cormorant is a legendary fisherman. Cormorants are used in China to fish for men. The bird dives and swims from the fishing boat of its master attached to a long leash with a ring around its neck. The bird fishes but cannot swallow. It is then relieved of its catch by the fishermen upon return to the boat. The bird then fishes again. Such is the prolific nature of the cormorants success rate as a fisherman that it catches more than enough for its master and (ultimately) for itself.

2. Cormorants are also found on inland waters in the north. (See for example: 'Cormorant Island' in 'Swallows and Amazons' by Arthur Ransome. This is based upon an actual rocky islet on Lake Coniston).

3. Some of the debate as to the origins of the cormorant-like image in the zoomorphic interlace of the Lindisfarne Gospels is described in an essay by Janet Backhouse in 'Birds, Beasts and Initials in Lindisfarne's Gospel Books'. This essay is published in 'St. Cuthbert, His Cult and His Community' edited by Gerald Bonner, Clare Stancliffe and David Rollason. In it Backhouse outlines a view of Rupert Bruce-Mitford that the Lindisfarne Gospel images are based entirely on Mediterranean models and lack any influence from local wildlife. Backhouse strongly disputes this view.

4. Similar bird images also appear in the Durham Gospels. This is a brilliant but more fragmentary Gospel Book currently preserved in Durham Cathedral library. It is one of a group of manuscripts associated with the community of Cuthbert and is believed to have a Lindisfarne provenance. There is debate as to whether the Durham or the Lindisfarne Gospel is the earlier book. The establishment of this priority would also establish who first devised the Cormorant interlace ornament. Whatever the priority however, it does not detract from the view that this decorative motif was influenced and inspired by the birdlife of the Northumbrian islands.

5. The Cormorant is the more likely model for the scribe. The Shag (also depicted) moved north in numbers in a later historic period.

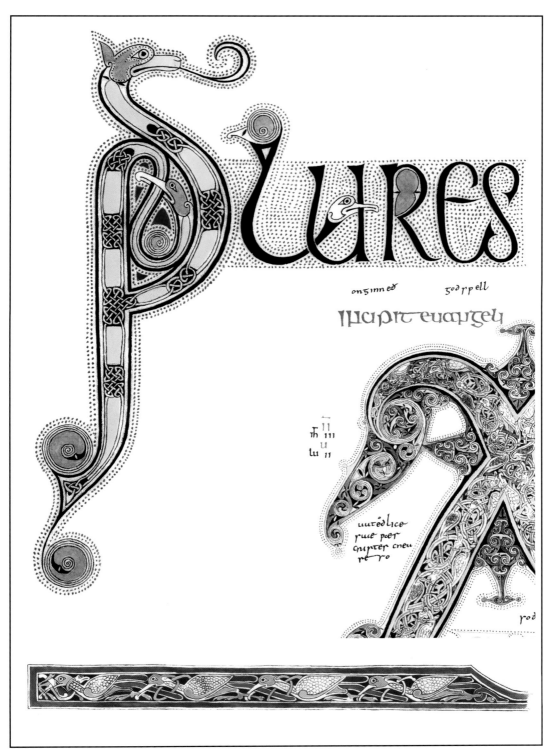

Three studies from the Lindisfarne Gospels of zoomorphic interlace used in illuminated lettering and in borders. *Studies by Tina Pooley and Susan Moor*

THE WILDCAT

Eadfrith was very careful in drawing the animals and birds which fill the decoration of the Lindisfarne Gospels. Many of the animal bodies have been made longer. They are twisted and shaped in stylised ways. The shapes intertwine and blend into magical patterns.

Within the rhythm of the pattern it is sometimes hard to find which animal is which. Some people can see the Osprey among the intertwining birds. This beautiful bird would be common in Northumbria in the days of Cuthbert. Others see dogs in the interweave. These dogs would be hunting dogs used by Northumbrian nobles in the chase. Such dogs would be long and lean and fast, like the greyhounds, whippets and wolf hounds of today.

When one creature clearly emerges from the surrounding whirl of pattern, Eadfrith paints it with detail and accuracy. We have seen this with his picture of the eagle of St. John. We have noticed how he draws and colours the feather patterns on the Cormorant. One other creature clearly emerges. It is the wildcat.

The cat appears on the opening page of St. Luke's Gospel. The page centres on a beautiful illuminated initial letter. A border runs down the right hand side of the page. It is filled with an interlace of bird forms. When the border reaches the bottom of the page it turns left to run along the base before ending abruptly in mid page. It is only when we reach this point that we see that the pattern ends with the head of a wildcat. This cat has been perfectly observed. It has the breadth and power of a wildcat head – a domestic cat is much more delicate. It even has carefully drawn cat whiskers! Looking back the whole border now appears to be the elongated body of the wildcat. A more vivid imagination might even see the animals and birds of the interlace as being part of a huge meal which the cat has eaten!.

There are two other cat forms to be found within the framing lines of a letter 'M' in part of St. Matthew's Gospel.

Wildcats were common in Anglo-Saxon Northumbria. Cuthbert will have encountered them many times on his missionary journeys. When he was a young monk at the monastery of Melrose he used to make a special point of visiting villages far away on 'steep and rugged' mountains. He would sometimes stay there for up to a month. Even towards the end of his ministry in the two years Cuthbert served as Bishop, the saint continued his travels to the remote uplands and 'mountainous and wild regions'.

These 'rugged' and 'wild' regions were home to the wildcat. Cuthbert will have seen many. It seems right that this cat of the rugged wilderness should feature in the Gospels dedicated to a saint who more than any other was determined to take the love of Jesus to these wild and remote locations.

NOTES ON THE WILDCAT

1. The wildcat is still to be found in Scotland though it has been extinct in England for many years.

2. The wildcat is a particularly fierce creature and features strongly in Scottish folk law. The motto of the Clan Chattan is "Touch not the cat but a glove".

3. Kate Tristram, of Marygate House on Holy Island, believes that the shape of Ospreys can be discovered among the zoomorphic border interlace.

4. This large and spectacular bird plucks fish from the waters of loch and river with its talons. It is a master of flight and wonderful to watch.

5. The Osprey was extinct in Britain for many years but was famously reintroduced to Lock Garten in Scotland. There are now a number of breeding pairs established including one in the Lake District.

6. Hunting with hounds was well established among the nobility of Anglo-Saxon Northumbria and beyond. The main quarry would be deer. Strains of rangy hunting dogs were developed, the fore runners of today's specialist breeds. The whippet of course became a favourite of the miners of the Great Northern Coal Field. It gave much pleasure in cut-price home grown racing in local communities. (Whippets often feature in the paintings of Norman Cornish the celebrated mining artist.)

7. A celebrated wildcat crag of the Scottish Borders is to be found in the valley of the River Irthing north of Gilsland on the Roman Wall.

Study of a detail of the wildcat border and an illuminated initial from the Lindisfarne Gospels.
Studies by Susan Moor

THE DUN COW

In 793 A.D. Viking raiders from over the seas arrived in their longboats to attack the community at Lindisfarne. Monks were hurt and killed and the raiders stole many things of great value. There were further raids.

The monks realised that they were no longer safe on their island. They took with them their most precious possessions and fled inland. These included the incorrupt body of their saint, housed in a special wooden coffin-reliquary, and the great Gospel book dedicated to his memory. They wandered extensively throughout the north. Many of the resting places of the coffin are now marked by churches dedicated in honour of St. Cuthbert. At one point they attempted a crossing to Ireland. This was thwarted by divine intervention. A storm jeopardised the boat and the precious Gospel book was lost in the sea. After much prayer the monks were led to the book lying unharmed on the sand after an exceptionally low tide.

After many wanderings they came to Chester-le-Street where they stayed for 113 years. Here the shrine of Cuthbert became very important and was visited by two English Kings.

Viking incursions deeper inland forced the community of Cuthbert to move again. They travelled first to Ripon and then moved further north. When they reached the ridge at Wardenlaw the coffin became too heavy to move. The monks knew that God was trying to speak to them. They prayed and slept.

During the night one member of the community had a dream. In the dream he was told that the new resting home for Cuthbert and his people was to be 'Dunholme'. Unfortunately when the monk shared his vision, no-one knew where 'Dunholme' was. At that moment a woman passed by searching for her lost animal, a light brown or 'dun' cow. It had strayed, she said, to Dunholme. The monks were delighted to hear the name. They asked her the location of Dunholme and the woman was able to direct them. It was not far away.

The monks of the community of Cuthbert went to lift their saint's coffin. To their delight they found it now rose easily from the ground. This confirmed their sense of a divine leading. The monks quickly made their way to the hill now known as Mount Joy. From there the community first saw the beautiful peninsular hill of Dunholme, covered in woodland and enclosed on three sides by the River Wear.

They walked along the riverside until they came to a place where the river could be forded. They crossed the river and climbed a steep path to a place of open grassland amid the trees. Here they built a chapel of tree boughs to house the precious coffin of the saint.

NOTES ON THE DUN COW

1. The story of the wanderings of the Community of Cuthbert is most completely chronicled in the writings of Simeon of Durham. Simeon's narrative brings us to the point of the crisis for the travellers at Wardenlaw. He tells us of the weighty coffin which cannot be raised. He recounts the details of the visionary dream which identifies Dunholme as the intended destination of the community. This however is the full extent of the story as told by Simeon. There is no woman. There is no missing beast. There is no dun cow.

2. A good deal of this much loved and oft-repeated story would appear to be the colourful trappings of later legend. The north east of England, which was at the heart of historic Northumbria and later shared a common industrial heritage, has always had a strong sense of regional identity. One aspect of this is that the region has retained and cherished its culture of folk tale. The tale of the dun cow is one of the most popular stories

3. The essence of folk tale is the oral tradition. The troubadour retells the story. In doing so he unconsciously edits. Popular aspects of the story are amplified. Less interesting parts diminish. The story crystallises only when it is written. Additions to the tale may have occurred at any stage of this oral development. An attractive and simple retelling of the crystallised tale is to be found in "Folk Tales of the North" by Frederick Grice.

4. There is much circumstantial evidence to support the legend to be found in Durham City. The hill of Mount Joy is so named and overlooks the city from the West. From this vantage point the visitor can see the whole peninsular. There is a clear pathway into the city. The modern concrete structure of the Kingsgate footbridge follows the line of the ancient ford, by which the Community of Cuthbert traditionally first crossed.

5. Historic alleyways lead from the riverbank to the Palace Green in front of the cathedral. The first of these is known as Bow Lane. The continuation is Dun Cow Lane. At the point of intersection stands the church of St. Mary-le-Bow. This church is said to be the ultimate successor to the original chapel of boughs erected by the monks.

6. Dun Cow Lane runs alongside the north wall of the cathedral. A bass relief of a milkmaid with her cow is incised into the exterior stonework of the Chapel of Nine Altars and overlooks the lane. Robert Surtees in his monumental "History and Antiquities of the County Palatine of Durham" comments, "The well known story of the dun cow, the accidental conductress of the wandering monks, is entirely unknown to the early writers. Its best evidence is, perhaps, the sculpture on the cathedral, which may after all as probably have given rise to the legend, as the legend to the sculpture".

Durham Cathedral on its wooded peninsular across the River Wear. *Photograph Robert Cooper.*

THE SERPENT AND THE SAINT

The shrine of St. Cuthbert in Durham became for a time the most celebrated sacred destination in England and a centre of national pilgrimage. King Cnut, the last Danish king of England made a celebrated pilgrimage to the shrine, walking barefoot and tonsured from Trimdon to demonstate to his Anglo-Saxon subjects that he respected their culture.

A series of magnificent buildings replaced the original humble chapel of boughs erected by the monks. These buildings culminated in the magnificent Romanesque cathedral built by Norman power which now dominates the Durham peninsular. As the buidings grew more grand so the shrine within became more opulent. Unfortunately in the competitive spirit which developed between centres of pilgrimage some of the stories which were attributed to the shrine and the power of the saint grew increasingly fanciful and bizarre. Here is one from Simeon of Durham.

One day a pilgrim named Osulf found himself attacked by a serpent as he lay sleeping in a field by the wayside. He awoke suddenly to find a serpent had twisted itself around his neck as he slept. Osulf grasped the serpent. He pulled it from his neck and dashed it to the ground. Within a moment the serpent recovered and twined itself again around Osulf's neck. Osulf seized the snake throwing it once more to the ground. The serpent attacked him again. Every time it tried to wrap him in its coils. Osulf grew desperate. He threw the serpent onto his fire, or into the stream but each time it returned stronger than before. Even when he took his sword and cut pieces from the snake it reassembled and attacked again. As Osulf fought, so the serpent grew larger and stronger. Osulf realised that this was a supernatural beast and this was a spiritual attack. He hurried to complete his pilgrimage to the church in Durham where St. Cuthbert's body lay. As he entered the door of the church the serpent fell from his neck.

This was not the end of Osulf's problems. After spending time at the shrine of the saint he left the church. As he did so the serpent, which had lain waiting for him, attacked again. Osulf retreated into the church. He was safe only when under the protection of the saint. Osulf gave himself to prayer. He prayed for three days and nights. This time when he emerged in the morning the serpent was gone and Osulf could journey onward in peace.

Osulf had been a difficult man who had not behaved well. After this salutory experience he amended his ways and knew the forgiveness of Christ in his heart and life to which this pilgrimage experience to the shrine of the saint had led him.

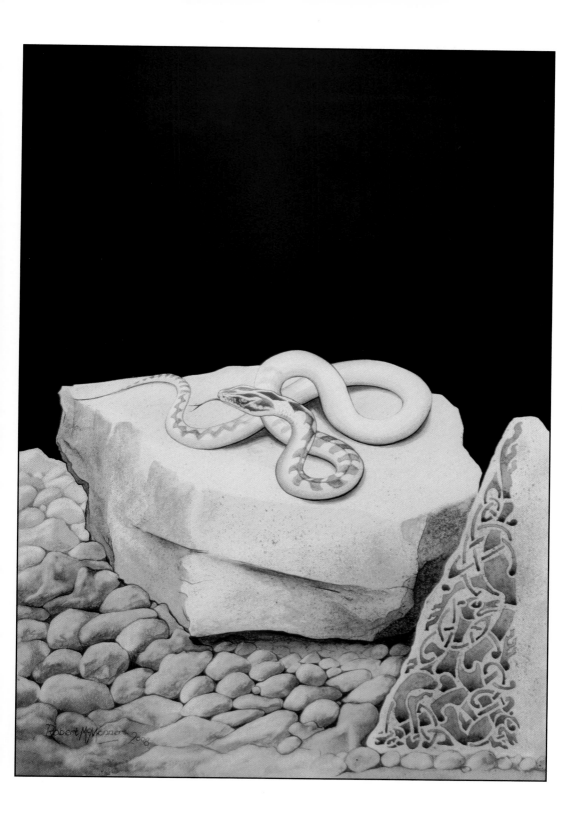

NOTES ON THE SERPENT AND THE SAINT

1. This story is in Simeon of Durham's account of the life of the community of Cuthbert. It is one of many miracles he records as having been associated with the shrine of the saint.

2. The story is attributed to the period around 1071 A.D. This is the time of the Anglo-Saxon abbey church at Durham which housed the shrine of St. Cuthbert before the building of the great Norman cathedral.

3. Osulf is referred to as an 'ill conducted individual' who is compared to other visitors to the shrine of St. Cuthbert who have not known how to conduct themselves.

4. The story carries resonances of the worm legends of County Durham. The Lambton Worm tale is the most celebrated. This story also describes a serpent who when severed by a sword can regenerate. The protagonist Sir John Lambton eventually succeeds in killing the serpent by standing in full flowing water as a battleground. This has the effect of bearing away sections of the serpent as they are cut off, before they are able to regenerate. Sir John is advised on his battle strategy by a local witch, as he too recognises the supernatural dimension in the serpent.

5. The serpent of the worm legends are much larger creatures than that described by Simeon. Another celebrated local serpent is the Sockburn Worm. This creature is said to have been despatched by Sir John Conyers using as a weapon the 'Conyers Falchion', a broad 'scimitar-like' sword, currently preserved in Durham Cathedral Treasury.

The unadorned grave of St. Cuthbert behind the high altar in Durham Cathedral.
Photograph Robert Cooper.

THE TALE OF THE WEASEL AND THE SHRINE

In the eleventh century custody of the tomb and shrine of St. Cuthbert came under the control of one Elfredus Westowe, more commonly known as Alfred. He was something of a showman. He would regularly exhibit clippings from the hair and fingernails of the incorrupt body of the saint. According to Alfred these were still growing. Alfred would demonstrate their miraculous properties to credulous onlookers. In short Alfred was a bit of a rascal.

How someone of Alfred's character was given responsibility from the abbot for the most celebrated shrine in England is something of a mystery. He did have one saving grace however; Alfred was passionately committed to the shrine of Cuthbert and to the saint. He enjoyed a remarkable intimacy with the spirit of Cuthbert, who would appear to him in visions in times of crisis.

One day Alfred, having completed his ministrations to the body of the saint, made to shut the lid of the coffin. In doing so he made a minor error. The coffin shifted slightly on its plinth. This revealed a small hole in the corner of the coffin at its base. The coffin had become very old and some of the corner jointing had weakened. The smallest of gaps had been created and was now left exposed. This gap was so tiny that it was barely noticeable to the human eye, but on that day another eye was watching.

A mother weasel had been able to nest in the abbey by exploiting a hole in the fabric. Some cleaning or restoration had discovered and filled the hole. The mother weasel had been unwittingly evicted. She was expecting to give birth to her young at any moment. She needed a new home. And she needed it quickly. The anxious eye of the weasel alighted upon the small gap in the base of the coffin.

The weasel was able to secret herself unnoticed under the fabrics that covered the coffin, and slip through the inviting gap. The opening was near to the feet of the saint. Here the weasel nested and had her young. Though she was a wild creature, she was not unaware of the sanctity of her location. The little animal was careful to confine her activity to the foot of the coffin and not to soil or touch the vestments which wrapped the body of the saint.

The spirit of the saint was nonetheless disturbed by the intrusion. Alfred had been detained in another region, so Cuthbert appeared in a vision to his clerk requiring his return. When Alfred came back he searched the abbey for the offending creature. There was no sign of the weasel whose presence had disturbed the saint. He never thought to look in the coffin itself. It took a further prompting from the saint to produce the sacred examination needed.

When Alfred found the mother weasel with its young in the foot of the coffin he was furious. He would have harmed them in his rage had not the gentle spirit of the saint spoken once more into his heart. Cuthbert urged mercy and kindness to the little animals. When Alfred looked once more upon the weasel he saw that she too had been sanctified by her proximity to the saint. The weasel did not run or fight or bite. It had been infused with a spirit of gentleness.

Alfred was able to lift the creatures from the coffin. He stroked the weasel's back and the young nestled in the palm of his hand. By now quite a crowd had gathered. They were charmed by the little weasels. They saw the gentle demeanour of the creatures and marvelled at their beauty. Folk began to realise what had happened. They all longed to stroke and caress the mother and her young. All praised God and gave thanks for their patron saint, whose holiness continued to bless all whom he encountered, even in death.

88

NOTES ON THE WEASEL AND THE SHRINE

1. This tale appears only in the writings of Reginald of Durham, who chronicles the history of the shrine and community of Cuthbert. It is only one of numerous miraculous and remarkable episodes he recounts linked with the shrine.

   Many of these seem to be pretty fanciful and would appear to be calculated to increase the prestige of Durham as a centre of pilgrimage during a credulous age.

   (Reginald also writes extensively about St. Godric of Finchale)

2. The Bishop at the time of the tale was Bishop Edmund (1020-1041).

3. This tale is set at the time of the great Anglo-Saxon abbey church, a successor to the original humble church erected by the monks who first climbed the river-girt hill of Dunholme with the body of their saint. When the magnificent Norman cathedral was built the Anglo-Saxon church was so thoroughly demolished that not a trace of it remains.

4. Elfredus Westowe is a controversial character in the history of the shrine of Cuthbert. He appeared to operate on the margins of legality and propriety. His zeal for the cause of Durham as a centre of pilgrimage knew no bounds. He is 'credited' with the theft of the bones of Bede from their resting place in Jarrow to add to the sacred relics in Durham.

5. The elaborate and opulent shrine of Cuthbert disappeared at the time of the Reformation and Dissolution of the Monasteries when according to the antiquarian Canon James Raine the tomb was 'ransacked'. The original coffin reliquary is remarkably preserved and can be seen in the Cathedral Treasury.

6. Some of the more intimate vestments which wrapped the body of the saint appear to have remained undisturbed, both by legendary weasel and Henry's commissioners, for it was not until the opening of the coffin in 1827 that the beautiful pectoral cross was discovered among the remains of the robes nearest to the breast of the saint.

The Chapel of the Nine Altars built to accommodate pilgrims to the shrine of St. Cuthbert.
Photograph Robert Cooper

AFTERWORD

In retelling of the tales of Cuthbert and the Animals I have sought to revisit the life of the saint from a different perspective. The tales are ancient but the underlying sentiments speak directly to us today. We have much to learn from a spirituality that works with the grain and rhythm of the natural world and rejoices in the whole of creation.

I also hope that the tales retain a devotional flavour and that the reader may see, in the colours of the illustrations, a refraction of that radiant life which inspired them.

Most of all the stories must be interesting. A tale, to be worthy of the name, must be worth the telling. There are many stories which got away. In the end the tales that were included more or less chose themselves as, once heard, they continued to resonate.

Many folk have helped and encouraged this venture. The wonderful book 'Two Lives of St. Cuthbert' by Bertram Colgrave *(Cambridge University Press, 1940)* has been a constant inspiration and widely used for source material. The Rev'd. Dr. Alan Bartlett and the Rev'd. Dr. Gavin Wakefield fuelled my enthusiasm for this period of church history. The Rev'd. Dr. Ian Stockton, The Rev'd. Stuart Hill, Mrs Val Hughes and the congregation of the Parish of Monkwearmouth responded favourably to early ventures. Rob Marshall has asked me to lead or guide Lindisfarne pilgrimages. My thanks also to my current colleagues the Rev'd. June Talbot and the Rev'd. Peter Robson and to the congregation at St. Gabriels for listening patiently to 'oft told tales'. Thank you to Robert Cooper for his beautiful photographs and helpful advice, to Penny Minney for fine translations of Reginald of Durham and to Christine Rodgers for reading an early draft of the text. Thank you also to Susan Moor and Tina Pooley for their superb calligraphy and to Carol Pye who typed some of the text and to Gillian Wales and Stefa McManners who proof read the text. Joan Williams and the staff of the cathedral library in Durham and Kay Eason and the library staff at the Literary and Philosophical Society in Newcastle, have all been very helpful. My wife Gina has been endlessly patient, encouraging and practically supportive. My collaboration with my brother Robert, who has produced the most wonderful illustrations, was suggested by our late mother Winifred Mc Manners, to whom this book is dedicated.

The artist, Robert McManners, would like to acknowledge the inspiration he has derived for his illustrations and over the years from such wonderful wildlife artists as Charles Tunnicliffe, Ken Lilly, Winifred Austin, Archibald Thorburn and James Alder.

As well as wildfowl and seabirds, the margins of Lindisfarne are home to many waders. Lindisfarne is an important centre for the Golden Plover.